CON

WHY A LEXICON?

In the past 20 years or so, the consumption of fish and seafood in the UK has soared. Species that were once rarely seen on restaurant menus – monkfish, sea bass and scallops, for instance – are now commonplace, and the British are discovering and developing a taste for these newly popular varieties. But while most people are experimental in their choices when eating out, that intrepid approach has largely failed to cross over to the way they shop for fish to eat at home; instead, they stick to familiar choices like cod, haddock and plaice that hold no fear and spring no surprises, whether in terms of preparation method, flavour or texture.

That's why we decided to put together this lexicon; to create a definitive guide to the texture, aroma and taste of almost 100 key species on sale in Britain, as well as carving out a new vocabulary that fully captures the immense diversity and complexity of those fish. In doing so, we hope to give readers both the tools better to understand the wealth of different fish available to them, and the confidence to enjoy them more.

A crucial factor in that enjoyment is an understanding of what makes for good fresh fish, which is why we've included a guide to the factors that determine its quality, as well as a checklist of what to look for when shopping for it (page 124). Equally, while the majority of the species covered in the lexicon are wild, we've also included a significant proportion of farmed fish as we believe that, if carefully and responsibly managed, such fish farms produce a quality product.

This project has been something of an adventure for us; as far as we are aware, the character of fish has never been analysed in quite this way before, and certainly never presented in this type of comprehensive lexicon format. In the tastings that formed the basis of the lexicon entries, we've been fortunate in being able to draw on the knowledge and expertise of some of the many talented people who work for us. But we've also looked beyond the confines of Young's in shaping its content; the involvement of chef, restaurateur, fishmonger and founder of FishWorks Mitch Tonks has been central to its development. This book reflects the commitment to promoting the enjoyment of fish that he shares with us.

Wynne Griffiths,
Chief Executive, Young's Seafood

Fishing is a way of
life across the world…
eating fish enhances life

FINDING THE FLAVOUR

When conducting tastings for this lexicon, it was important that the fish and seafood were prepared in a way that would showcase their flavours as clearly as possible. As a result, all of the species were cooked using one or two different methods, both of which were kept as simple as possible.

Fish was cut into fillets, then fried, unseasoned, skin side down in a non-stick frying pan with a splash of a hot non-flavoured vegetable oil. Thin fillets were fried for about three minutes. Thicker fillets were fried for four to five minutes, before being transferred to a hot oven for up to five minutes, so that they cooked throughout. Aside from oysters, which were tasted raw, all seafood and crustacea were steamed, or in the case of crab and lobsters, boiled in plain water. Cooking times varied widely according to size: large seafood such as crab took 15 minutes, with prawns steaming for around five minutes.

In the following pages you will discover varieties of fish, some familiar, some less so, but all worth trying at least once. This lexicon should serve as a starting point – but there's no substitute for conducting your own tasting!

THE TASTING TEAM

Tasting panel, left-right: Rob Olivant (Young's), Serge Nollent (Young's), Simon Rilatt (Young's), Guy Miller (Young's), Mitch Tonks (fishmonger, chef and founder of the FishWorks restaurant group) and Tim McLaughlin-Green (head sommelier at FishWorks)

ARCTIC CHAR

Salvelinus alpinus

Although there is plenty going on in Arctic char's aroma – a blend of buttery chicken skin, the green, chlorophyll hit of steamed broccoli as well as something of the yolkiness of a boiled egg – the taste of its pink flesh is much less assertive, with a very delicate, clean character that makes it a prime candidate to pair up with other, more robust flavours. The texture is similar to that of freshwater trout: fine, small flakes, but with a faster moisture release that results in a higher tooth-pack* rating.

*The tendency of certain fish to take on a dense, almost sticky texture when chewed, causing it to adhere lightly to the front and back of the teeth and to become 'packed' into the indentations of the bite surface.

BARRACUDA

This solid, muscular fish has an aroma of roast pork,
similar to that of tuna. The flavour is quite different,
however – dominated by a mild green bean note
with a bolder, peppery character around the fat line.
At first bite the texture is quite resilient, but the
rapid release of its moisture means that the flesh
becomes crumbly (a little like pork) quite quickly,
leading up to a fairly dry mouth-feel, similar to that
of rich tea biscuits.

Sphyraena barracuda

BARRAMUNDI

Lates calcarifer

FARMED

Barramundi's aroma is pungent, with an intense, mushroomy character, and the taste is equally assertive, with a bosky depth that's reminiscent of a forest floor or a freshly cut block of peat, especially in the darker flesh around the fat line. Those autumnal flavour notes make it a good partner for ingredients that are around at that time of year, such as cep and girolle mushrooms; nuts, especially almond; and woody herbs like rosemary and thyme or dill, with its faintly caraway character. It's also assertive enough to stand up to robustly flavoured wines. The texture is not unlike sea bass: firm, with a moderate amount of moisture and a crumbly mouthfeel.

BASA
(PANGASIUS)

FARMED

Fairly unassertive in character, basa has a low-key aroma similar to the water in which spring greens have been cooked. The texture is quite open and light, the small flakes yielding moisture easily. Although the flavour – reminiscent of freshly picked new potatoes or mushrooms – remains fairly one-dimensional with most cooking methods, that neutrality makes it a good blank canvas for other, more highly flavoured ingredients. To coax more taste from the fish try grilling, which brings out deeper flavour notes, such as cashew and roast chicken, in the flesh around the fat line.

Pangasius hypophthalmus

BASS
SEA

Dicentrarchus labrax

WILD

Notes of rocky earth and fresh, iodiney sea air combine to give wild sea bass a complex aroma, and the taste in both skin and flesh is no less sophisticated: clean but intense, with elements of fresh seaweed and the ozone hit of rock pools just exposed by a retreating tide, with great length of flavour. The flakes are arranged in a distinctive snake skin pattern, and their texture is substantial and fairly oily, with an initial burst of juice that disperses to give a satisfying, chewy mouthfeel.

FARMED

While its appearance (grey-white, with a slight speckling) is fairly nondescript, at its best, farmed sea bass has a wonderfully multi-layered smell and flavour. The former is a mix of oceanic freshness, the green, chlorophyll character of samphire or river reeds and a hint of mussel-like iodine balanced by a deeper nuttiness suggestive of roast chicken or sweet potatoes. The flavour, most of which is held in the skin, matches the aroma for complexity – a blend of the brininess of oysters and barnacles and the earthiness of potato skins, balanced by a spicy sweetness. Smooth, small flakes give the flesh a firm but delicate mouthfeel.

BREAM
GILTHEAD

Sparus aurata

WILD

The skin of wild gilthead bream takes on an extraordinary appearance once pan-fried – almost reptilian, its surface rough with what look like desiccated, transparent grains of wheat. This texture gives the skin an enjoyably crisp mouthfeel, the perfect contrast to the uniform richness of the juicy flesh, each slender flake of which is separated from the next by a slick of oil. While the skin has the flavour and aroma of pork crackling, the flesh is more delicate, with notes of the burnt, crispy edges of the white of a fried egg and the dark meat of a chicken, especially around the fat line. There's a difference in flavour between the loin and the tail, too, the latter carrying more of an oily depth.

FARMED

Combining the sweetness of vanilla essence and the deep, savoury quality of crab or crayfish shells, farmed gilthead bream has a richness of aroma that is not reflected in its flavour, which tends towards a dilute marine oiliness (although the taste of the skin is a little more substantial, with notes of roast chicken). The flesh is pale grey with some hairline black veining and, while it can't compare with the complexity of farmed sea bass in terms of flavour, it does share something of that fish's texture: firm but delicately flakey, with a moderate amount of juice, most of which is a consequence of the distinct and (for a white fish) unusually oily fat line, which sticks to the flesh, rather than the skin.

BREAM
THREADFIN

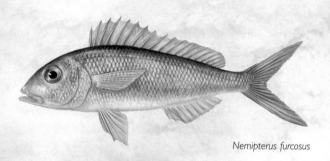

Nemipterus furcosus

Few fish are as easy to eat as threadfin bream – the flesh is so succulent that it's almost slippery, releasing moisture at a constant rate when it's in the mouth. The texture is short, breaking down into soft filaments, rather than individual flakes, similar to the way a ball of mozzarella tears apart. The aroma carries a suggestion of bacon rashers that have been cooked wrapped around a roasting chicken breast, together with a note of the crispy edge of a fried egg. That caramelised egg white flavour is present in the flavour, too, though with a slightly more pronounced sweetness.

BRILL

The first bite of brill gives up a blink-and-you'll-miss-it hint of diluted acidity, swiftly giving way to a more low-key, consistent flavour like the caramelised edges of a fried egg (an echo of the fish's most noticeable aroma). The texture is firm, but not substantial, with a balanced moisture content and something of the turbot's subtle, gelatinous stickiness. Avoid eating the skin, which is rough and bitter.

Scophthalmus rhombus

CATFISH
SPOTTED (ROCKFISH OR SPOTTED WOLFFISH)

Anarhichas minor

Defined by starchy notes of well-boiled parsnips or floury potatoes, catfish's aroma is as mild as its flavour. The main impact it delivers is in its texture. White and muscular in appearance, with large, discrete flakes, the flesh gives a distinctly gelatinous and slippery mouthfeel, not unlike the fat you would find on a joint of meat. This distinctive character is a consequence of the thick layer of jelly that lies between skin and flesh. Cooked skin-on in a pan or under a grill, the skin is too moisture-saturated to crisp up; the fish fares better cooked slowly in a stew, which helps the jelly-like fat to break down a little.

CLAM
AMANDE (DOG COCKLE)

Displaying all the typical mollusc aromas – fresh seaweed, the salty smack of ocean spray – clams also feature something milder and rounder, a little like the smell of the crispy white edge of an egg as it's frying in a pan. Their tan-coloured flesh has a marshmallow chewiness, releasing a lot of juice and, while the flavour is rooted in that characteristically salty, rockpool note, it's given depth by an immediate sweetness as well as a more piquant suggestion of soft bacon rind. The slightly tooth-resistant texture and sweet/savoury taste make it a great match with spaghetti.

Glycymeris glycymeris

CLAM
PALOURDE

Ruditapes decussatus

The aromas of a British beach in high summer – hot
rocks, plus beached seaweed slowly drying to brittle
crispness along the tide line – define the smell of
palourde clams, though that savoury, umami
character is underpinned with a faint suggestion
of 'wet dog' mustiness. Take a mouthful, and there's
a slight but immediate sensation of sliminess, but
that rapidly passes to reveal a chewy texture at
the front of the flesh, while the meat towards the
back of the shell has a softer, more yielding quality.
From first to last bite there's a generous amount
of juice, the strong saltiness of which is balanced
by the flavour of the meat, which has a lobster
or scallop-like sweetness.

CLAM
RAZOR

Like palourde clams, but in a much more intense way, razor clams have a smell evocative of the aromas of a sun-baked British beach. Their long, linear shape gives them the appearance of mini squid and, at their foot, the meat is noticeably chewy, with an abrasive, sandy feel. Towards the centre of their length, that rubbery, gritty quality lessens; the flesh becomes tinged with green, and the flavour takes on a shellfish-like sweetness. At the tip, where the flesh is at its whitest, the texture is softer still – smooth and yielding, like a lychee – and the flavour has a sharp tang, a little like sour cabbage.

Solen marginatus

COBIA

Rachycentron canadum

FARMED

Cobia has the initial appearance of having large, even, discrete flakes. However, the texture is, in fact, quite confused, with an apparently random arrangement of flakes that vary significantly in size, some quite chewy, some pappy and soft, but all with an underlying graininess. The aroma is mild, with a slight vegetable or leafy greenness, and the taste is a mix of the juicy, roast pork or meat stock flavour notes of the dark flesh (which also has a faint burnt orange peel aftertaste) and the caramel, buttery, milky elements of the white.

COCKLES

Fairly tooth-resistant in texture, cockles have an underlying grittiness at their core that gives the smooth, mobile flesh a little more bite. The scent is mild, with an ozonic freshness that's close to the smell of raw cod, plus a deeper note suggestive of the burnt wood aroma of an extinguished match. There is a hint of dilute, almost floral sweetness to the flavour, but it's extremely mild – this is a seafood that definitely requires other, more dominant ingredients to give it some character.

Cerastoderma edule

THE CODFISH

No book on the subject of fish would be complete without reference to Atlantic cod. Famed for its snow-white, pearlescent flesh, large, succulent flakes and subtle but distinctive flavour, it has long been one of the world's favourite fish and an important, internationally traded commodity for many hundreds of years. Initially, it was preserved by natural drying in the sun and wind, either on cliffside rocks, 'klipfisk', or wooden frames, 'stockfisk' (both Scandinavian terms), or by being packed in rock salt (known as 'bacalhau' in Portuguese-speaking nations and 'bacalao' in Spanish-speaking nations). Today, modern preservation techniques such as refrigeration and freezing are also used but, as has always been the case, cod is preserved close to where it is caught and transported from those fishing grounds to reach markets all over the world. The UK is one such market – here, 90 per cent of the cod we eat is imported from northerly fishing nations.

In addition to wild-caught Atlantic cod, we have also included two worthy alternatives: farmed Atlantic cod and the closely related, wild-caught Pacific cod. These two alternatives offer interesting variances in flavour and texture that make them great ingredients in their own right.

As well as these 'true' cod species, we've featured other members of the Gadidae family – haddock, Alaskan pollock and saithe among them. While sharing some fundamental cod-like characteristics, these also offer rich and subtle differences in aroma, texture and flavour.

COD
ATLANTIC

WILD

Long the most popular member of the Gadidae family, cod is typified by its wonderfully firm flesh, the large, pearly-white flakes of which fall apart easily when cooked. A soft base note of floury potatoes, lifted by hints of sweet mustard and fresh peas, dominates the smell, and the flavour is unmistakable: an immediate sweet tang of dill, followed by a delicate, oceanic aftertaste. In the mouth, the flesh is moist and silky, but the dense, tight texture of the flakes provides a long, even chew. Cod's characteristically firm nature is particularly noticeable in just-caught examples, but the fish will tenderise in a day or two.

FARMED

Gadus morhua

Farmed cod's distinct aroma of whole milk is reflected in its flavour, whose first hit of lactic sharpness gradually softens to an intense, synthetic sweetness, together with a just-detectable taint of cod liver oil. Although the large flakes are densely packed, the flesh falls apart easily, but the fibrous nature of the flakes create a chewy texture – and, despite its juicy appearance, there's little moisture present to balance out that tooth-resistant mouthfeel.

COD
PACIFIC

Gadus macrocephalus

Another variant of the Gadidae family, Pacific cod
has particularly bright white flesh, which breaks into
firm, discrete chunky flakes. The aroma is dominated
by green notes, such as asparagus, cauliflower and
olive oil. Even more subtle in flavour than Atlantic
cod, the flavour has notes of freshly dug vegetables
and a faint ozonic tang.

COLEY
(SAITHE)

Dull white in colour, with a slight translucence and fine grey marbling, coley belongs to the same family (Gadidae) as cod, and shares its firm but tender texture and large, easily separated flakes, which means it's a worthy substitute for that fish (as well as haddock) in many dishes. The smell has a fresh, chicken broth quality with a suggestion of the seaside, and the flavour is clean but buttery, with a faint metallic aftertaste.

Pollachius virens

CRAB
EDIBLE

Cancer pagurus

BROWN MEAT

Savoury, with a slightly acid tang of canned tomato, the aroma of brown crab meat is rounded and deep. The flavour is sweet at first, with a very delicate saltiness, before a rich, piquant note of baked cabbage – particularly in its bubble-and-squeak incarnation – begins to emerge. The creaminess of the soft, wet, paste-like texture is given a little edge by a slight granular quality.

WHITE MEAT

The aroma of white crab meat is all about starch – first the damp coolness of cold batter on fried fish then, as the smell has time to develop a little, a strong, sugary suggestion of tinned sweetcorn. The taste is multi-layered: an initial fleeting burst of sweetness as the flesh releases its copious juice, followed successively by a bland neutrality and a faintly metallic, bitter note that lingers on as an aftertaste. Short and crumbly, the meat has a fragile, fibrous texture, falling apart in the mouth very easily.

CRAB
ALASKAN KING

Paralithodes camtschatica

Lift a piece of king crab to the nose and it seems to release its aroma in waves – first a meaty sweetness, then an ozonic seaweed freshness and, finally, the fermented starch smell of sake. The flavour of the predominantly white flesh is similarly multi-layered, featuring an earthy, estuarine saltiness, as well as the subtle vanilla and pork notes (especially in the pink-tinged meat close to the shell) more commonly associated with some warm water prawns. Although the leg is the only part of the king crab's body that yields up any meat, its different sections offer an immense amount of textural variety; around the knuckle it is foamy and mousse-like, while the limb itself is made up of a mix of thickish but tender linear flakes, plus bigger, springier sections that have a mouthfeel not unlike lobster.

CRAYFISH

Deep brick red without, pale white within, shelled crayfish have a delicate, slightly fibrous texture, their soft flesh releasing a lot of juice fairly rapidly, then becoming progressively drier. The mild aroma carries notes of chicken stock and the lightly savoury smell of peeled button mushrooms; both of these are reflected in the flavour, which shows a goose fat luxuriance as well as the umami-rich taste of fresh fungi, together with some sweetness. All of these elements are stronger in the more intensely flavoured redder flesh.

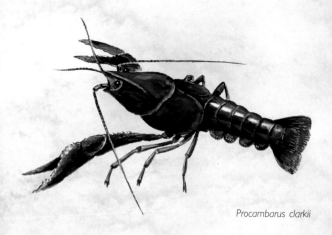

Procambarus clarkii

CUTTLEFISH

Sepia officinalis

Lightly sweet in aroma, with a suggestion of grilled bacon, cuttlefish has the same slightly tooth-resistant character as squid, the exterior of its flesh very firm, like well-cooked egg white, becoming more creamily silky towards the centre. The flavour has a delicate note of saffron, plus a suggestion of woody herbs, like thyme, underpinned by a lingering, prawn-shell richness. While incredibly popular in Spain and Italy, it's woefully underrated in the UK. That's a great shame, as it's affordable and easy to cook – it works particularly well in braises.

DAB

Dab's buttery, unctuous aroma isn't quite carried through to its taste, which is characterised by a subtle suggestion of cooked egg white. There is more intensity of flavour in the flesh towards the tail, which has an earthy depth, but it's insufficiently strong to overwhelm that consistent cooked egg note, which is carried through to a recognisably scrambled egg aftertaste. The flavour is firm, with a moderate level of moisture, and the bright white, slightly glossy flesh breaks into small, spindle-shaped flakes.

Limanda limanda

ESCOLAR

Ruvettus pretiosus

Escolar's aroma, with its meaty, roast beef character, signals the fish's similarity to tuna and, like that fish, the texture and flavour are robust enough to stand up well against assertive, sharp flavours. Its grey/white flesh is firm, breaking off cleanly in chunks, and its long, fine fibres give it a striated appearance, a little like the interior of a scallop. In the mouth, it has a substantial but yielding feel and a long-lasting richness. The flavour mirrors the aroma, with a strong suggestion of the fragrant fat on a succulent joint of roast beef. That intensity is balanced by the clean, fresh oily taste around the fat line, which has a slight hint of fishmeal.

FLOUNDER

The pepper and woody, cork-like notes that feature
in flounder's aroma neatly summarise its taste profile:
a bosky, almost musty depth, together with a spicy,
radish-like heat. Most of the flavour is concentrated
in the darker meat of the top fillet, rather than
the paler flesh of the more bland bottom fillet. The
texture is quite soft, the initial release of moisture
quickly dispersing to leave a dry, crumbly mouthfeel.
The rubbery skin is fairly fatty, with a greasy, almost
rancid butter aftertaste, so is best removed before
eating. Several of these characteristics – yielding
texture, peppery flavour notes, and an unappealing
skin, together with an almost translucent appearance
– are shared with plaice, making flounder a good
substitute if that fish is not available. To maximise its
appeal, it's best skinned and filleted, then fried, with
or without crumb or batter coating, and paired with
robustly flavoured veg such as spinach or kale.

Platichthys flesus

GREY MULLET

Liza ramada

New leather and a deep, unrefined sweetness close
to muscavado or palm sugar are the predominant
notes in the aroma of grey mullet. The flavour
echoes some of that nubuck character but, instead of
sweetness, it's balanced by the muskiness of a newly
cracked hazelnut shell, and a strong suggestion of
tomatoes grilled just short of being charred. A fine
mesh of strong fibres and a fairly low level of
moisture results in a chewy texture.

GURNARD

Sharing the same firm, muscular texture as monkfish, gurnard has a fairly neutral, understated aroma. That restrained character is echoed in the muted flavour, which carries notes of mussel and clam, as well as a just-perceptible hint of almond. The flesh tends towards dryness, but not unpleasantly so.

Eutrigla gurnardus

HADDOCK

Melanogrammus aeglefinus

Like cod, haddock is one of the most highly regarded of the Gadidae family, with an ozonic aroma that encapsulates the salt water from which it is fished – fresh, with notes of seaweed and the tang of clean, beachy air. That oceanic character is followed through on the flavour, which is delicate, with a suggestion of seashells and fresh spring greens. The texture is lean but succulent, the flakes of the spearmint-white flesh quite compact but readily breaking apart. If possible, haddock should be bought and cooked skin-on – it's thin, and easy to eat.

HAKE
CAPE

Smelling of a kind of starchy freshness, like clean washing or boiled new potatoes with the skin still on, Cape hake has a lush but uncomplicated taste, combining the sweet sleekness of double cream with a hint of salt. The texture is delicate – soft, like white bread soaked in milk – but without any mushiness, and the thin skin is very easy to eat. Such subtlety of flavour and richness of texture make it a good contender for light, dressing-like sauces.

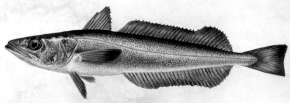

Merluccius capensis

HAKE
EUROPEAN

Merluccius merluccius

With the starchy aroma of baked or fried potatoes, European hake has a light but multi-layered flavour, featuring a soft lemon balm note, a warm, vanilla sweetness and a green, fern-like element, as well as a suggestion of mushroomy earthiness. The milky, grey/white flesh has a good level of juice, creating a yielding, melting mouthfeel.

HALIBUT[†]
ATLANTIC

Although very clean and subtle in aroma, Atlantic halibut has an assertive flavour, reminiscent of a very good rare steak. The texture of the ivory flesh reinforces that steak-like nature: muscular and substantial but with a delicate tenderness and a high level of moisture that provides a notably silky mouthfeel.

Hippoglossus hippoglossus

† Atlantic halibut is among a few species included in this lexicon that, owing to their stock status, should currently be regarded with particular caution; these are indicated with this symbol †.
For more information, turn to page 128.

HALIBUT
GREENLAND, MOCK OR BLACK

Reinhardtius hippoglossoides

Although not the same species as Pacific halibut, this flat fish is so named for its similarity in appearance. Once a fillet is cooked, there is a noticeable amount of shrinkage in the flesh, causing it to curve upwards at its edges. The aroma has starchy notes of boiled potatoes, lifted by a hint of fresh seaweed, and the taste is very mild, a little like milk pudding. Juicy to the point of wetness, the flesh is very delicate, with an aerated, moussy texture – in fact, it's so soft that if it is pressed to the roof of the mouth with the tongue, it will disintegrate.

HALIBUT
PACIFIC

Much like the smell, a barely-there green note of
steamed fresh soya beans, halibut's flavour is quite
unassuming, with a light neutrality suggestive – just –
of sunflower oil. The texture is more unexpected; the
bright white flakes appear big and succulent but, in
the mouth, are smaller and closer, with a sticky
rather than juicy quality, and break down slowly to
give a long chew and a high tooth-pack rating. It's a
satisfying, if not rich, eat, and the texture and low-key
flavour of the fish means that it handles the addition
of punchy ingredients such as citrus or fennel, as well
as buttery sauces, very well. As the skin is very fatty,
it's best not eaten.

Hippoglosus stenolepis

HERRING

Clupea harengus harengus

Shimmering with green and silver, herring's iridescent skin and sleek form make it a particularly good-looking fish. Its high oil content is responsible for its pungent aroma, which has a distinctively petrolly, resinous character, together with a strong tannic note, like the inside of a well-used teapot. That same oiliness contributes a fresh, anchovy-like saltiness to the fish's flavour which, combined with the delicate seawater character of the skin and the mild, white pepper spiciness of the flesh, makes for a complex taste. The texture is unctuous and lush and, although small, filament-like bones are liberally distributed through the flesh, they are so fine and pliable that they can be eaten without concern. Good flavour matches include strong herbs like coriander, sharp vinegars, punchy salsas – anything with a piquant character that can cut through the oil.

HOKI
NEW ZEALAND

Hoki's yellowy-white, slightly translucent flesh gives off a subtle but distinctive smell of boiled greens and unsalted butter, together with a slightly beefy, Bovril-like note – and there's a faint suggestion of sardine there, too. In the mouth, the assertiveness of some of those aromas gives way to a rather more bland flavour, a sweet blend of buttery cake mixture and a rounded milkiness; this is a fish that would handle the addition of herbs or spices very well. The flesh is creamy rather than juicy, and has a chunky, substantial texture that leads to a longer chew.

Macruronus novaezelandiae

HUSS †
(SPURDOG, ROCK SALMON OR DOGFISH)

Squalus acanthias

Huss's almost tubular middle-section results in a
log-like fillet shape, giving the appearance of a hunk
of snake meat – dark on the exterior, a paler beige
within. Bland and indistinctive, the aroma has
a faint suggestion of the water in which vegetables
have been cooked, and the taste is similarly
unassertive. The texture lacks structure, giving
a smooth, very wet mouthfeel, like poached
egg or pressed tofu.

JOHN DORY
(ST PETER'S FISH)

John Dory's aroma is very light, with subtle hints of fresh seaweed and boiled potatoes. Its flavour is marginally more robust, featuring milky notes of plain omelette, most of which it owes to its thin, crunchy and very easy to eat skin. The flesh is noticeably more bland, but compensates with a very elegant texture – firm and smooth, with discrete flakes and a pleasant, low-key stickiness.

Zeus faber

KINGCLIP

Genypterus capensis

Very white and glossy, with some translucence, kingclip flesh is firm, compact, and tremendously moist, yielding up its sweet, watery juice slowly and steadily, no matter which part of the fillet from which the flesh is cut. While the aroma carries a suggestion of hard boiled egg white, the flavour is fresh and sweet, like the uncooked white of a very fresh egg. Its firm but luscious nature makes kingclip perfect for pan-frying, and the flesh is also sufficiently robust in texture to work well in curries, casseroles and soups.

LANGOUSTINE
(DUBLIN BAY PRAWN OR NORWAY LOBSTER)

The langoustine's slender body and claws mean that it yields up comparatively little flesh, but the flavour more than repays the labour-intensive business of shelling them. The aroma carries echoes of lobster, along with the marine, spumy freshness of a windswept beach and an underlying starchiness, not unlike clean washing just unpegged from the line. Smooth and velvety in texture, the flesh has a rounded, elegantly sweet and rich taste, with notes of Jerusalem artichoke. The flavour is released steadily, with no peaks or troughs, and there is no aftertaste to speak of.

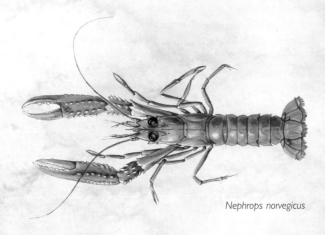

Nephrops norvegicus

LING †

Molva molva

Ling's bright white flesh has a texture that's firm but balanced by a marshmallow-like lightness, a consequence of the irregular pattern in which the flakes are arranged. The aroma has a sharp, malt vinegar tang, with a slight vanilla undertone, and that honeyed note is reflected in the flavour, which has a mild shortbread sweetness and a clean, rounded aftertaste. Although the skin is thick and clings to the flesh quite doggedly, it makes for good eating. Braises and soups are perfect ways in which to use ling, as the flesh is robust enough not to fall apart during the cooking process.

LOBSTER
AMERICAN

Lobster claw, tail and brown meat all have different characteristics. The brown meat is incredibly rich, with a creamy consistency similar to foie gras and pronounced flavour notes of crustacea as well as a subtle suggestion of saffron. In contrast, the tail flesh is much more compact, with a mouthfeel of firm calves' liver – slightly resistant to the tooth but releasing plenty of juice at first bite. The aroma is reminiscent of steamed cabbage or seaweed, but the flavour is powerfully mineral, conjuring up the iodine crispness and cool, salt-sprayed stone of freshly exposed rockpools. That green cabbage aroma is given off by the claw meat, too, but in a lighter, cleaner way, and the flavour has the intense sweetness of a well-sugared cup of tea. Its smooth, liver-like texture intensifies towards the tip.

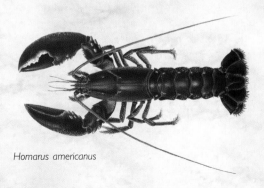

Homarus americanus

LOBSTER
ROCK

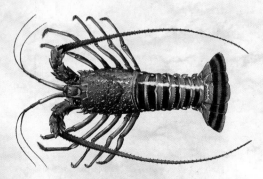

Panulirus cygnus

Characterised by beachy, iodine-laced notes of seaweed and seaspray, the aroma of freshly cooked rock lobster is fleeting, although it does develop a suggestion of almond as it cools. The flavour is rich, especially in the flesh closest to the shell, with elements of saffron and a slightly bitter, metallic note that's balanced by a nutty depth and a gradually released sweetness. Initially juicy but firm with a slight crunch reminiscent of a ripe apple or pear, the texture of the pure white flesh becomes increasingly tender as it's chewed.

LOBSTER
SQUAT

Highly perfumed, squat lobster gives off an aroma
of the sea – salty, clean, with the iodine freshness
of rockpools. The flavour is mouth-filling but delicate,
with a coolly spicy saffron note and a suggestion
of crustacea. When chewed, the slightly slippery
flesh releases considerable juice – it feels a little
like eating a mandarin segment – and the firm
but yielding texture, especially in the leg, is similar
to that of spider crab meat.

Munida rugosa

MACKEREL

Scomber scombrus

Distinguished by its sleek, streamlined shape and silver-blue skin marked with dark blue bands, mackerel is a fish that particularly repays being eaten spankingly fresh, before its high oil content starts to spoil. Its aroma is light and oceanic, reminiscent of fine green seaweed, and its predominantly pink flesh is succulent, with discrete flakes that are almost chicken-like in texture. Although there's a high level of oil, it's balanced by generous amounts of juice, which help disperse it in the mouth, and the flavour is delicate, with a low-key coal dust or driftwood aftertaste that gives a pleasant minerality.

MACKEREL
SPANISH, NARROW BARRED

Firm and muscular, Spanish mackerel has an incredibly flaky texture very similar to tuna, each individual flake sufficiently large and discrete as to be more like a segment in appearance. The generous quantity of gelatinous oil that separates each one gives the mouthfeel a rich, almost sticky quality, a nice counterpoint to the flesh's compact density. The aroma has a mellow, roast beef character, and some of this is echoed in the flavour, which is reminiscent of a joint of beef (on both the tender interior and the caramelised exterior), with a hint of ground white pepper spiciness, as well as a metallic, iron-like minerality on the aftertaste, much like medium-rare beef.

Scomberomorus commerson

MAHI MAHI

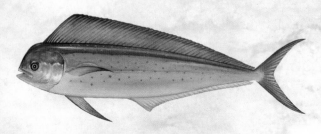

Coryphaena hippurus

Similar in appearance and colour to swordfish,
the meat of mahi mahi has a light aroma
suggestive of chicken broth. The flavour is far
more multidimensional, with the sweet citrus
notes of a satsuma or clementine balanced out
by the delicate, clean oiliness of its velvety fat line.
The flesh, which is composed of unusually large,
noticeably discrete flakes, has a texture similar to
the meat from a chicken thigh and is packed with
a moisture that's steadily released – bite in, and
the fish delivers the same mouth-filling succulence
of a juicy piece of well-rested roast lamb.

MARLIN

With an extremely substantial, robust texture, marlin
can seem more meat than fish. Its densely packed
flesh and very pale pink, almost white tone gives
it an appearance not unlike veal, but once in the
mouth it's exceptionally close to steak – an
immediate juiciness giving way to a chewy, fibrous
feel with flakes so supersized they are more like
segments. In fact, if blindfolded, it would be very easy
to mistake it for beef. The aroma is an amplified
version of the smell of keta salmon (citrus, a little fish
oil, as well as the crisp edge of a fried egg), but the
taste is pure sirloin steak – caramelised on the
browned exterior, a faint metallic hint on the tender
pink interior, together with a slight acidic note
reminiscent of grilled tomatoes.

Makaira mazara

MEGRIM

Lepidorhombus whiffiagonis

Megrim is uniformly bright white in colour, with
a deeply savoury, vegetal taste. In common with
many flat fish, this flavour is most pronounced on
the bottom, thinner fillet, which carries an additional,
earthy element. The flavour profile is reflected in the
aroma, too, which features notes of boiled leek or
cabbage. After an initial burst of moisture, the flesh
gives a fairly dry mouthfeel, with a texture that is
more fluffy and lightly fibrous than flaky. This is
in marked contrast to the thin skin which, when
cooked, has an appealingly crunchy, bacon-rasher
crispness, and a rounded, caramel sweetness.

MONKFISH

Nutmeg, cinnamon, Demerara sugar – the individual notes of monkfish's aroma give it a sweetly spicy character, a little like mulled wine. The flavour is much less forceful, being mild, slightly sweet and quite fleeting, but it's that shortness in taste that makes it one of the most versatile fish available, good for roasting, baking, frying and grilling. The muscular texture is another factor in its adaptability, as it's very forgiving, with a dense but juicy mouthfeel and great consistency, delivering the same level of moisture and robustness in every bite.

Lophius piscatorius

MUSSEL

Mytilus edulis

If any one seafood distils the essential nature of the sea, it's the mussel. That oceanic character is especially pronounced in its aroma – a blend of surf and fresh seaweed, with an underlying saffron-like spicy note. The initial mouthfeel is silky, the exterior of the mussel having a smooth texture, like a rich mousse. Bite in, and the feel shifts to a rich, almost egg-yolk like liquidity, releasing flavour notes of fennel seed and a mild brininess. The interior is firmer, with a chewiness comparable to bacon rind.

MUSSEL
GREEN LIPPED

Perna canaliculus

With the briny, seaweedy aroma of sun-baked rockpools, green-lipped mussels have a smooth texture, similar to a chewy nougat (though, if roe is present, it takes on a grainy character). The lip in particular is yielding but, in a way that's similar to squid, also offers a little resistance to the teeth. The flavour is one of instant and intense sweetness, which lingers for some time.

OYSTER
NATIVE

Ostrea edulis

Noticeably smaller than Pacific oysters, natives have a round, flat shell. While they have the same overall oceanic smell and taste of Pacific oysters, their character is more complex, with flavour notes of fresh seaweed as well as the suggestion of citrussy and faintly metallic elements. Although the texture isn't quite as creamy or juicy as that of Pacific oysters, this multi-layered, fine flavour means that they are considered to be the superior of the two types. As natives are a protected species, they may only be harvested outside of their spawning season, which runs from the start of May to the end of August; natives eaten close to the spawning season can be 'milky' with a cloudy juice, a softer, pulpier texture and a less fine flavour.

OYSTER
PACIFIC OR ROCK

With a large, long, deeply cupped shell, Pacific oysters have a flavour and aroma that sums up the sea, like the ozonic tang of ocean spray or the briny freshness of newly exposed rock pools. Take a first sip of the juice in which the oyster sits, and the taste is salty; take a second, and it's much purer and lighter – this is the fluid held within the folds of the oyster itself. When chewed, the meat has an unctuous, sweet character. Unlike native oysters, Pacific oysters are available all year round.

Crassostrea gigas

PLAICE

Pleuronectes platessa

ICELANDIC

With its ivory white flesh and loose, velvety smooth, borderline watery texture, the appearance of Icelandic plaice suggests a fairly bland eat. Only the aroma, which has a lively, peppery piquancy, like sprouted seeds, gives a hint of this fish's more complex flavour profile, which combines a spicy hit of coriander seeds and bean sprouts with a deep, treacle sweetness, as well as a suggestion of toasted hazelnuts. The black skin does not make good eating, so is worth taking off, but the softer white skin is tender, so can be left on.

UK

With an opaque white flesh that takes on particular brightness during its peak season, plaice has a green aroma, like fresh garden peas with mint. The flavour is unassertive, just a clean, faintly lemony acidity, and the texture is very fine, the flakes almost imperceptibly small. Combined with relatively high moisture, the delicate texture leads to a meltingly soft mouthfeel, similar to that of lemon sole, especially in its crumbly, shortbread-like finish. In contrast, the skin can be a little bitter, with a sandpapery, coarse feel on the dark side of the fish (the white side is much smoother), and its fatty nature gives it a greasy, almost margarine-like taste.

POLLACK
ATLANTIC, CORNISH

Pollachius pollachius

Like cod, Atlantic pollack is a member of the
Gadidae family. It has a fairly thick skin, the nutty
Amaretto-like aroma of which is particularly
highlighted when pan-fried. Compact in appearance,
the white flesh breaks into discrete, delicate flakes,
each one with a glossy sheen and a slippery
mouthfeel, thanks to a high moisture content. The
taste is a perfect balance of the skin's faint bitterness
and the flesh's carrot-water sweetness, which builds
steadily in the mouth, leading to a distinctive
aftertaste, reminiscent of marrowfat peas.

POLLOCK
ALASKAN

Alaskan pollock is another member of the Gadidae
family but, while it shares cod's shape and has a
similar texture, its faintly mustardy, milky aroma is
more muted. The same can be said for its flavour,
which features notes of sweet green herbs
(predominantly parsley), and a delicate creaminess.
The flesh is white with a faint beige tinge and, while
firm, is softer and smoother than cod – more like
crab meat, in fact – so offers less resistance to the
tooth. Most Alaskan pollock sold in the UK has had
its fat line removed – if it's still present, it will add an
oily flavour note (but not texture) to the fish.

Theragra chalcogramma

POUTING
(POUT, BIB OR POUT WHITING)

Trisopterus luscus

Pouting isn't the kind of fish that repays being served simply, with no adornments. Just like the smell, the taste of this member of the Gadidae (cod) family is almost entirely neutral, whatever character it does have being a consequence of the light, buttery flavour of its thin skin rather than its white, semi-translucent flesh. Such anonymity needn't be a disadvantage; it takes on more strongly flavoured ingredients very well, and the texture (firm, not overly juicy, breaking easily into large flakes) makes it a great choice for fish cakes or Thai curries.

PRAWNS

The world's oceans support hundreds of different species of prawns (also known as shrimps), both cold and warm water varieties. For the purposes of this lexicon, a representative selection of the most commonly available species on sale in Britain has been made.

The cold water prawns featured in this lexicon are wild caught in the Barents Sea, close to the Norwegian island of Spitzbergen, as well as in fisheries around Iceland, Greenland and northern Canada. The bouquet shrimp variety, which has also been included, is found mainly off the coasts of western France and southern Eire, as well as (in much smaller numbers) the south west coast of England. Cold water prawns can be bought either single or twice frozen. Single-frozen prawns are caught from inshore fisheries, landed raw, then cooked, peeled and frozen before being sold. Twice-frozen prawns are generally caught in sea fisheries, frozen whole on board to maintain freshness then, when landed, cooked, peeled and refrozen.

Warm water prawns, also known as tropical shrimp, are found in the seas of the Tropics in both eastern and western hemispheres, primarily those around India, China and Central America.

Several of the most popular varieties of tropical prawns are also now farmed in huge quantities, particularly in Indonesia, India, Ecuador, Honduras, Panama, Vietnam, Colombia, Mexico and Madagascar.

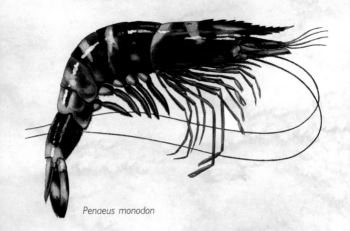

Penaeus monodon

FARMED

A good-looking crustacean with a glossy sheen and, once cooked, a deep coral colour, black tiger prawn (the name refers to its inky striped appearance before cooking) has a neutral, slightly salty aroma and a strongly sweet flavour that carries (improbably but not unpleasantly) a suggestion of new leather. The flesh is very succulent, with a juiciness that remains in the meat rather than dispersing quickly in the mouth. Good flavour carriers, they are perfect for salads – a classic prawn cocktail with a punchy Marie Rose sauce works particularly well.

ORGANIC FARMED

The origins of organic black tiger prawns are evident in their smell, which is dominated by a note of riverbed silt, as well as one of damp linen and a gentle mustiness suggestive of library books. That earthy character is echoed in the flavour, too; particularly in the meat of the head, which is subtly underpinned by a mild, vanilla sweetness. In the tail, that flavour balance is reversed, the meat being dominated by a strong, fruitier sweetness, its musty note far more downplayed. Although there's a good level of juice, the flesh itself has a pappy, cotton wool texture, although it becomes marginally firmer towards the tail.

PRAWN
BLUE

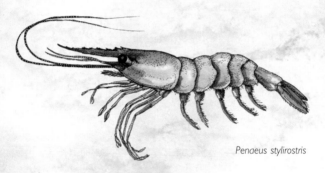

Penaeus stylirostris

FARMED

Best bought raw, these prawns from the Coral Sea
are vivid blue and have a paper thin shell that gives
off a perfumed, vanilla aroma. It also lends an
intensely sweet, caramel character to the flesh, which
is balanced by a dry, spicy peppery quality, similar to
a very well-cured Iberiço ham. The shells are so
insubstantial that they can be left on for eating but
are most commonly peeled off so that the texture
of the flesh – yielding, but with a slight crunchiness,
a little like broccoli florets – can be fully enjoyed.
Grilling or barbecuing makes the best of the prawns'
size, texture and taste.

PRAWN
COLD WATER

SINGLE FROZEN

Smelling sweet and sea-fresh, single-frozen cold water prawns don't give up as much juice as double-frozen, but compensate with a creamier, more compact flesh that delivers a much more complex and intense spectrum of flavours: gentle, spicy notes of radish and mustard seed, greener herbal elements of sorrel and rocket, together with a richer, crab-like base note.

DOUBLE FROZEN

With a subtle, oceanic aroma, double-frozen cold water prawns are very delicately flavoured – there's just a suggestion of salt and seawater, backed by an underplayed sweetness. The texture is a little like a very ripe pear, extremely juicy, but with a slight resistance to the tooth. When defrosting, the best way to preserve their low-key taste is to put them in a bowl in the fridge; resist the urge to defrost by pouring water over them, as this will wash away what flavour there is.

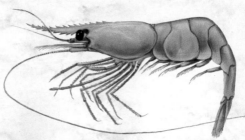

Pandalus borealis

PRAWN
COMMON

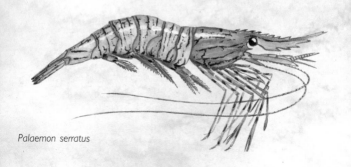

Palaemon serratus

Common prawns are very beautifully marked with
a delicate, coral-coloured marbling. Their shells are
so thin that they can be left on for eating, adding
a pleasantly crunchy counterpoint to the firm flesh,
which has a texture not unlike beef fat – resistant to
the bite at first, then yielding. The aroma is intensely
oceanic – sweet, salty and fresh – and the flavour is
reminiscent of potted shrimps – honied and buttery,
with a subtle suggestion of spice and a rich, lingering
aftertaste. Their flavour and texture means that they
are the perfect type to use in a pint of prawns, or to
briefly deep-fry, shell-on.

76

PRAWN
FRESHWATER

FARMED

A plastic, synthetic note, and the muddy siltiness of damp leather or river water – there's no mistaking the aroma of these large, freshwater prawns. The flavour itself is pretty bland – it's only at the tip of the tail, where the white flesh warms to a rosy pink, that a faint, almost citrus sweetness comes through, followed by an aftertaste that echoes the synthetic character of the aroma. As the texture is so firm and dense, this is a prawn that provides a substantial, enjoyable eat, but which needs to be paired with strong flavours to balance out the neutrality of its taste.

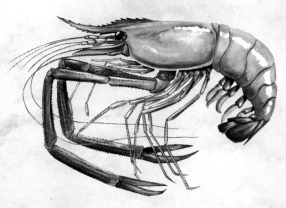

Macrobrachium rosenbergii

77

PRAWN
INDIAN WHITE

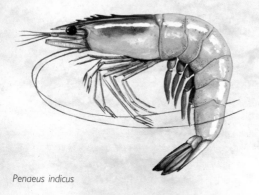

Penaeus indicus

Notes of bonfire smokiness, roast nuts and cabbage combine to give these large, whole prawns (sometimes called tropical crevettes) an intense, complex aroma (much of which is carried on the shell), and that's followed through in the powerful flavour, which has both a savoury depth, a little like pork, as well as a vanilla, honied sweetness. The texture is muscular and juicy, making it a very good choice for grilling or barbecuing.

PRAWN
TIGER (CAT TIGER, SWORD OR SPEAR)

Once shelled and cooked, the cat tiger prawn coils into a distinctive, fat disk. Its slightly translucent flesh makes it look similar to a lychee, especially given its pearly white colouring, touched in places with very pale pink. The aroma is delicately fishy but the flavour is markedly different, with a suggestion of steamed asparagus and a faintly metallic, saffron aftertaste.

In the mouth, the slippery, gelatinous exterior gives way to flesh that is surprisingly firm, with a crisp, Chinese water chestnut texture that breaks apart in distinct chunks when bitten into. Its understated taste means that this is the ideal curry prawn, as it takes on strong, spicy flavours very well.

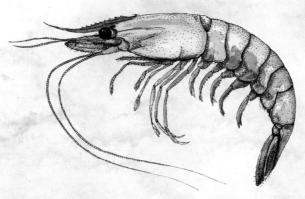

Parapenaeopsis hardwickii

PRAWN
WHITE LEGGED, KING

FARMED

Although king prawns have an earthy, pond-water aroma, this is carried through in a much more diluted form in their flavour, which features muted notes of field mushroom and fresh popcorn, lifted by the hint of leafy, herbal greenness towards the end of the tail and the sweetness of the plentiful juice that's released on first bite. The texture is succulent, with a meaty, veal-like character, giving the flesh an appealing al dente feel. The combination of robust texture and muted flavour makes them perfect for stir fries, fish pie and soups, and they pair up with Asian herbs and spices particularly well.

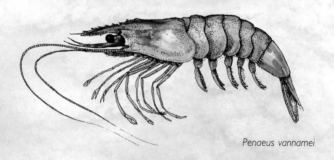

Penaeus vannamei

RAY [†]

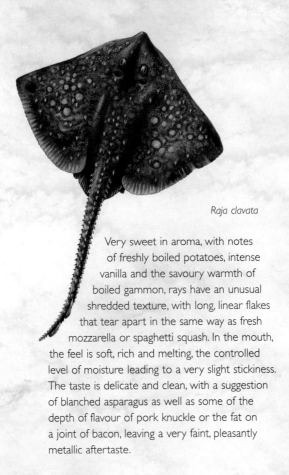

Raja clavata

Very sweet in aroma, with notes
of freshly boiled potatoes, intense
vanilla and the savoury warmth of
boiled gammon, rays have an unusual
shredded texture, with long, linear flakes
that tear apart in the same way as fresh
mozzarella or spaghetti squash. In the mouth,
the feel is soft, rich and melting, the controlled
level of moisture leading to a very slight stickiness.
The taste is delicate and clean, with a suggestion
of blanched asparagus as well as some of the
depth of flavour of pork knuckle or the fat on
a joint of bacon, leaving a very faint, pleasantly
metallic aftertaste.

REDFISH†

Sebastes marinus

Neutral in aroma, redfish is almost as unassuming on the palate, the only discernible note in its flavour profile one of very faint sweetness. Its flesh is white with just a faint blush of pink, and the large flakes are firm and gelatinous to the point of being rubbery. That chewy character is toned down when the fish is cooked without its skin, which also results in the flesh losing some of its jelly-like nature, despite the fact that the fat line is attached to the flesh, rather than the skin. Fish as low-key as this needs to be paired with big, robust flavours to bring it to life – try it in spicy curries or fish pie.

RED MULLET

A fish with an incredibly intense taste, red mullet has
a deep, savoury aroma, a blend of roasted crustacea
shells, particularly crab or lobster, along with a
sweeter note of orange peel. The flavour matches it
for concentration of flavour, with the earthiness of
new Jersey Royals and iodine freshness of seaweed
and salt spray, together with an edge of saffron-like
spiciness, especially in the dark meat. The skin adds
another flavour element, with the taste and crunchy
texture of blistered chicken skin. This makes a great
contrast to the soft but firm character of the clearly
defined flakes, which are smooth and dense, like
chicken oysters, but with a light oiliness that keeps
the mouthfeel luscious.

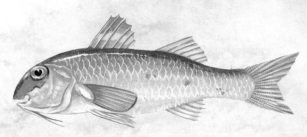

Mullus barbatus

RED SNAPPER

Lutjanus erythropterus

Mildly gamey in aroma, with a fatty scent that isn't reflected in its mouthfeel, red snapper has a springy elasticity, its well-defined and elongated flakes arranged in distinctive whorl patterns. The flesh is juicy and, in line with its smell, has a slight duck note, bolstered by a suggestion of roast chicken in the thick skin; for the best flavour the two – flesh and skin – should be eaten together. The fish has a noticeable fat line, which means that, along with the milder white flesh, there is plenty of dark meat, too, which contributes to its slightly metallic aftertaste.

SABLEFISH
(BLACK COD)

Also known as black cod (although it's not a member of the Gadidae family), sablefish has a light, starchy aroma, and a robust, mouth-filling flavour that features both a sweet, artichoke-like note and an oily undertone not dissimilar to that of mackerel. The just off-white flesh has a rich, lightly oily quality, and the large, discrete flakes have a smooth, delicate texture that's initially firm but yielding, but which gives way to a crumbly, biscuity texture as the flesh breaks down in the mouth. This fish is a substantial eat, and works well with assertive herbs and spices that play against its oily character — try rubbing it with chermoula before roasting.

Anoplopoma fimbria

SAILFISH

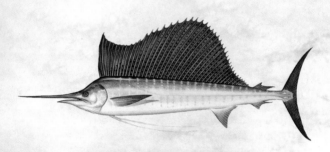

Istiophorus platypterus

The aroma of sailfish is unmistakeable – possibly
uniquely for the fish world, it has the same burnt
electric filament, friction smell of the underside of
a Scalextric car that's just been raced along the track.
Happily, the flavour is rather different, a sugar/salt
balance between an apple sauce sweetness and
a monosodium glutamate type of savouriness, the
latter having an umami-driven moreishness similar
to soy sauce. The texture is firm and dense, balanced
by a moderate amount of tangy, slightly bitter oil.

SALMON

One of the most versatile fish available, salmon works beautifully with virtually any cooking method. Grill, fry, roast, poach, smoke, bake or barbecue it – however it is prepared, its unique flavour and silky, rich flesh deliver reliably good results.

Instantly recognisable by its distinct colour, which varies from dusty pink to bright apricot orange, salmon encompasses a wide variety of species. For the purposes of this lexicon, we have selected two types of the native British species, Atlantic salmon – the first type being the widely available farmed variety, the second its organically farmed equivalent. We have also chosen a number of the wild-caught Pacific Ocean species, all commonly available from British fishmongers and supermarkets. While these fish are all very closely related, there are interesting differences in flavour and texture between them.

SALMON
ATLANTIC

FARMED

Salmo salar

There's no mistaking Atlantic salmon's unique flavour – rich, savoury/sweet but clean, its high oil content giving it a satisfyingly juicy mouthfeel and a skin that crisps nicely when pan-fried. The aroma carries piquant notes of orange peel, something that is coincidentally mirrored in the colour of the flesh, which leans towards the warmer end of the salmon-pink colour spectrum. Separating easily, the discrete, curved flakes have a luscious, silky quality towards their centre; this high moisture content is most apparent when the fish is cooked through, which causes the fat membrane that separates each flake to melt back into the flesh. The flakes break down easily in the mouth and the oil disperses quite quickly, to leave a drier-textured flesh.

ORGANIC FARMED

Strikingly bright apricot in colour, the flesh of organic salmon has a dense, compact texture, with an initial juiciness that gives way to a pleasantly crumbly mouthfeel. The aroma has an earthy intensity, like fallen autumn leaves, and the flavour is similarly autumnal in nature, with rounded, mellow notes of chestnuts balanced by some mild, orange-peel acidity.

SALMON
WILD ALASKAN, KETA

Although it's possible to detect a number of different elements in keta salmon's aroma – lemon, fish oil, the smell of warm milk just coming to the boil, as well as a suggestion of something metallic – they're all fairly faint. That subtlety is reflected in the flavour, too. It is unmistakably of salmon, but in a very underplayed way, dominated by a creamy note that morphs into a slightly metallic aftertaste. The texture of the flesh is dry, with a high tooth-pack factor; this is a fish that benefits from the addition of a rich, fatty sauce. Keta salmon is particularly prone to releasing a white, curd-like protein when cooked; it's not great on flavour, but is harmless.

Onchorhynchus keta

SALMON
WILD ALASKAN, PINK

Onchorhynchus gorbuscha

Unlike its farmed cousins, wild pink salmon is a leaner, more muscular fish that carries significantly less flesh and is consequently most commonly used for canning. It carries the same savoury/sweet flavour notes of Atlantic salmon, but in a much more subdued form. Instead, it's dominated by an oily, generically fishy flavour that benefits from being paired up with herbs or spices. The texture of the true salmon-pink toned flesh is less unctuous than many other salmon species, with a compact structure that releases little juice when chewed. This leads to a denser, drier mouthfeel with a high tooth-pack rating.

SALMON
WILD ALASKAN, SOCKEYE

Bright red when raw, and a deep, coral pink when cooked, sockeye salmon owes its intense colour to the mainstay of its diet, shrimps. The aroma is quite subtle, a combination of a chlorophyll-like element, similar to the water in which greens have been boiled, and a slight suggestion of raw chicken. The taste is similarly low-key, with traces of leafy green veg as well as a savoury, shellfish note. Dense and tightly packed, the flesh is composed of straight, rather than curved, flakes that don't break apart easily, and the mouthfeel tends towards dryness, with a high tooth-pack rating.

Onchorhynchus nerka

SARDINE

Sardina pilchardus

Despite their very high oil content, much of which
is held in the skin, sardines don't give an overly slick
mouthfeel; most of the oil is released on the first
bite, dissipating quickly to leave a pleasantly dry,
crumbly texture. The aroma has a cool metallic note,
as well as a suggestion of aubergine. This is carried
through in the flesh, which has an intense sesame
nuttiness (the result of all that oil) along with a
smokey aubergine note, reminiscent of Middle
Eastern chargrilled aubergine dishes such
as babaganoush. The flesh can be light or dark and,
although plenty of small bones are distributed
throughout it, they are filament-thin, so are scarcely
noticeable when eaten.

SCALLOP
KING

Milkily transculent when raw, pure opaque white
when cooked, king scallops have a unique texture,
with long, thin, soft but densely packed fibres that
give each one a striated appearance. The mouthfeel
is melting, with a creamy, almost foamy quality, a little
like a marshmallow. The aroma has a caramel
sweetness; that mellowness is carried through on
the flavour, but is given an added layer of complexity
with a hint of ozonic, seaweedy freshness. The roe
(sometimes called coral, on account of its warm,
orange colour) has a distinctively iodine-like, piscine
taste, and a slippery, elastic texture; the bigger the
roe, the silkier the mouthfeel, though the bitterness
of the iodine flavour note can become quite
pronounced in larger examples.

Pecten maximus

SCALLOP
QUEEN

Chlamys opercularis

In contrast to the caramel sweetness of king scallops, queen scallops have a milder, more vanilla-like, honeyed aroma and a full-bodied, sugared flavour with a slight hazelnut note. The texture is firmer, with a long-lasting, rich mouthfeel and a more obviously stranded structure.

SHRIMP
BROWN

Smelling sweetly of an ozonic blast of fresh sea air, brown shrimp pack a lot of flavour into their small forms, with notes of salted caramel and the mild acidity of the flesh of a green apple that has browned on exposure to the air. The texture is juicy and soft, a little like the tender inner leaves of cooked sweet cabbage, with the tooth-packing character of chicken breast. The sugared flavour and yielding texture pair up well with spaghetti with garlic and parsley.

Crangon crangon

SILVER SMELT †
(GREATER ARGENTINE)

Argentina silus

Silver smelt's bone structure makes it difficult to fillet and therefore it is generally used in mince or soups instead – a pity, as it has a fantastically delicate flavour. When whole, its sleek, torpedo-like body and pale, burnished skin give it the appearance of a large, silver mackerel. The muscular flesh is very white, with a texture that's not unlike Dover sole – firm, the flakes packed tight, with a good level of juice and a light, elegant mouthfeel. The flavour is wonderfully subtle, with notes of almond and a hint of oceanic freshness; that lightness is best showcased when the fish is lightly fried in butter, served with a squeeze of lemon juice and a scattering of parsley.

SOLE
DOVER

Strikingly elastic in texture, Dover sole is amazingly juicy, with small, tightly packed flakes. This close grain means that eating it is like taking a bite from a ripe pear or peach – the flesh is yielding, but sufficiently firm to hold a defined bite mark as it's bitten into. The aroma is piquant and savoury, like grilled bacon, and the flavour is rich and mouth-filling, with a hazelnut sweetness and depth.

Solea solea

SOLE
LEMON

Microstomus kitt

Although far less assertive in flavour than Dover
sole, lemon sole has a distinct shellfish taste,
particularly reminiscent of scallop and prawn,
together with underlying oaty biscuit notes and
a suggestion of sherry-like sweetness. The flesh
is not overly juicy and the small flakes mean the
texture is quite close but, once in the mouth,
the fish takes on a melting, velvety softness with
a faintly breadcrumb-like quality.

SOLE
SAND

Sand sole delivers handsomely on flavour – a rich, robust savouriness, like homemade meat stock, with a hint of cooked egg – but it is in its texture contrasts that it delivers the greatest impact. Crisp, with a slight grittiness, the skin provides a good foil to the rich, gelatinous, almost springy resilience of the firm flesh, which releases a clean, refreshing juice with each bite. This is a fish whose robust nature means it is quite versatile, allowing it to be cooked in a number of different ways.

Pegusa lascaris

SPRAT

Sprattus sprattus sprattus

With a light, marine freshness to their aroma, sprats
have a very delicate flavour, characterised by slightly
spicy notes of mustard cress and cumin, along with
a sweet, sesame taste that derives from their oil
content. Their small size (around 12cm on average)
and the softness of their white flesh means that the
latter can be easily peeled away (skin still attached)
from the spine to be eaten, or the whole fish can
be eaten ungutted, head and bones included.

SQUID
ILLEX

Meltingly tender, with a rich, mouth-filling texture similar to the kind of fat you would find on a joint of pork, just underneath the crackling, or the smooth, luscious flesh of a very ripe mango or avocado, Illex squid has no trace of the rubbery quality commonly (but unjustly) thought to define the texture of squid. The smell is light, reminiscent of the water in which eggs have been poached, with some of the ozonic, algal freshness of a windswept beach, and the flavour is equally subtle: pistachio with a hint of the mild lactic tang of fresh cream.

Illex argentinus

SQUID
LOLIGO

Squid has a reputation as being all about its texture, but the flavour can be wonderful, too – pan-frying is one of the best ways to bring it out. Cooked that way, it takes on a distinctively sweet aroma of toasted hazelnuts and toffee praline. Those sweet, nutty elements are echoed in the taste, which features intense notes of caramel chocolate and condensed milk with a slight oceanic saltiness. When cut with a knife, the pure white flesh yields like soft rubber. However, none of that rubbery quality is evident in the mouth – instead, it has the texture of a firm panna cotta and, although the characteristic halloumi-like squeak that it gives against the teeth would suggest a dry texture, the flesh gives out a considerable amount of juice.

Loligo vulgaris

SWORDFISH

Swordfish flesh is arranged in a distinctive whorl pattern (the larger the fish, the larger the whorl) similar to that of tuna, the skin having the lightly textured appearance of linen. In terms of its aroma it has more in common with meat than fish, with a strong suggestion of properly hung beef. There's a marked difference between the texture and taste of the meat at the whorled centre of a fillet and that at the edges. The former is pale, with a juicy, yielding character not unlike veal, and a lactic astringency that's suggestive of feta cheese or Greek yoghurt. In contrast, the flesh around the skin is softer, the wood-like grain exchanged for a soft, pressed tofu consistency. The flavour is more intense and there's also a sourish note of 'school milk' – that is, milk that's not quite off, but that has been left to stand in the warm for a time.

Xiphias gladius

TOOTHFISH
PATAGONIAN

Dissostichus eleginoides

Although it's possible to come across examples with a faint grey tinge, Patagonian toothfish (sometimes erroneously refered to as Chilean sea bass) generally has extremely white flesh, its smell combining a suggestion of the cooked white of a fried egg with a more savoury, browned note of crisp batter. The flesh is juicy, bordering on wet, each large flake coated with a layer of oil, a little like sea bass. Loosely packed, the flesh falls apart easily and, while the flakes have a slight fibrous quality, they're by no means tough – this is a fish that seems to melt in the mouth. The oiliness in the flesh contributes to a richness of flavour, somewhere between the lactic tang of soured cream and a sharper, citrus note; this taste becomes more pronounced as the fish cools – something that the looseness of the texture means happens quite quickly.

TILAPIA

FARMED

Slighty grainy, with small, close flakes, tilapia's flesh
has a compact structure, from which the moisture
dissipates quickly in the mouth. The aroma has a
background earthiness, a little like boiled floury
potatoes, and the flavour has a delicate creaminess
with a slight suggestion of caramel.

Oreochromis sp.

Onchorhynchus mykiss

FRESHWATER FARMED

Freshwater rainbow trout has very fine, discrete flakes – so discrete that they can be felt individually on the tongue. The texture is firm, with a reasonable level of moisture, which means that the flesh tends not to dry out in the mouth. Its freshwater status is reflected in both the aroma (clean and slightly earthy, like tilled soil, but lifted by a hint of lemon rind) and the flavour (which has a fairly flat, one-dimensional character, reminiscent of vegetables freshly lifted from the ground). The skin is thin enough to eat and echoes that loamy character, with a distinct taste of potato skin.

SEA FARMED

Smelling and tasting of fresh marine oil, with the addition of a hint of seaweed on the aroma and a low-key peatiness on the taste, farmed sea trout has extremely oil-rich flesh – the discrete flakes seem almost to have been individually glazed, to give a rich, smooth mouth-coating that's like olive oil in feel. Although the skin adds a deeper flavour note similar to crackling or roast chicken skin, it's the oil that remains dominant, even when it has dispersed a little to reveal more of the flesh's fine, delicate texture. The characteristic pink tone on the flank of rainbow trout becomes less pronounced when it has been sea-farmed; the fish will also be larger.

TUNA
ALBACORE

Thunnus alalunga

Like all tuna, albacore has a character that has much in common with meat, and is an excellent entry-level choice for those wary of fish. The flesh is even in texture, with a moderate amount of moisture that flees quite quickly. The aroma is reminiscent of roast pork chop, to which some sweetness is added by the caramelisation on the surface of the cooked fish. That pork chop note is also strongly present in the flavour, together with a citrus, acidic element that, just like rhubarb, causes the sensation of a tacky 'fur' on the teeth, as well as stimulating the production of saliva.

TUNA
YELLOWFIN

Displaying the typical tuna characteristic of very firm flesh arranged in distinctive whorls, like knots in wood, the texture of yellowfin is firm and juicy, its large flakes reminiscent of veal. It has a faintly acidic, clean smell that's reminiscent of pork crackling, with an underlying suggestion of the nuttiness of baked bread or brown butter. Some of those qualities are reflected in the taste, which is similar to roast pork or dark turkey meat. It's best cooked by briefly searing on both sides – the exterior should take on a pale, toasted oatmeal brown, while the interior should remain a rosy pink.

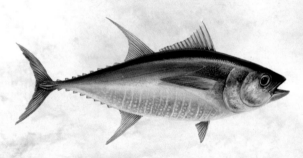

Thunnus albacares

TURBOT

Psetta maxima

WILD

Most of the turbot's subtle aroma, which features notes of potato skin and pork crackling, is concentrated in its skin, and is matched by an equally delicate seawater flavour balanced by a faint hint of sweetness. But although the flavour is appealing, it is its superb texture that has won it its 'King of Fish' reputation; firm and substantial, with a juicy elasticity, the white flesh breaks into large, even flakes with a silky, gelatinous character. The result is a luscious, almost sticky, pork trotter-like mouthfeel.

FARMED

Farmed turbot's aroma features a starchy sweetness, like sugary popcorn or the canola oil smell of fries from a fast-food outlet. Carrying through that sugared fragrance, the flavour has a caramel-like lactose character similar to burnt milk or gummy milk-bottle sweets. The texture is short and very smooth, with a tendency to break into large segments, a little like blancmange. The starchiness that is evident in the aroma is also a factor in the mouthfeel, giving the teeth a slighty furry coating.

WHELKS

Buccinum undatum

With the slightly charred aroma of burnt toast, whelks have a firm, rubbery texture, which gradually becomes a little more starchy and pliant, like overchewed chewing gum, the more it's worked in the mouth. Initially quite bland, the flavour then develops a hint of caramelised milk, followed by a more saccharin-like note of sweetness.

WHITEBAIT

Whitebait aren't full-grown examples of a particularly small species; they are fish that have been caught very young (usually herring and sprat fry). At first bite the texture is all about the crunchy dryness of the fish's crisp exterior, but then a slightly oily moisture is released, and with it, a mild sweetbread flavour of liver, together with an oceanic note of fried seaweed. Slightly larger examples with a little more flesh may have more of a generic fish flavour.

WHITING

Merlangius merlangus

Both sharp and savoury, the strong aroma of whiting
(a member of the cod family) is much like putting
your nose in a bag of salted and vinegared battered
fish and chips. The flavour is of full-cream milk –
intense at first, but very fleeting, and the texture
is soft and crumbly, like muesli or a flapjack.

WINKLES

Fresh, ozonic notes of seaweed and seaspray, together with the earthiness of wet sand and, very subtly, the mustiness of sodden wood, define the aroma of winkles. There is a marked contrast in texture between the flesh at the mouth of the shell and that deeper inside – the former is firm, with a rubbery quality, while the latter is much softer, almost paste-like, dissolving in the mouth quite easily. The winkle's delicate flavour is concentrated in the softer flesh, its subtle brininess a downplayed version of the oceanic character of mussels – and there's a suggestion of sweetness there, too, as if they have been oven-roasted or caramelised in a pan.

Littorina littorea

WITCH

Glyptocephalus cynoglossus

Delicate and juicy, with very small flakes, witch has a similarly smooth texture to silver smelt. The flavour is lightly sweet, like boiled milk or sticky rice, without the latter's cloying edge, and is less developed on the bottom, white-skinned side of the fish than on the darker top side. The sweet, gently starchy notes of the flavour are reflected in the smell too, but in a more dilute form.

ZANDER

Zander has a network of very thin grey/black filaments criss-crossing its surface, but cut into the fish, and the flesh is a much purer white. The aroma is savoury, with the smell of soft-boiled egg yolk and a certain cheesiness, together with a deeper note of browned meat. The thin coating of oil on its exterior gives an initial buttery mouthfeel but, as that moisture isn't present all the way through the fish, the flesh itself is quite dry, almost squeaking as it is chewed. This tendency towards dryness is amplified by the density with which the small, thin flakes are packed, along with each one's matt surface texture. The taste is extremely muted, with just a faint suggestion of the resinous character of fresh-cut wood. This neutrality makes it a great carrier for more assertive flavours.

Sander lucioperca

THE ART OF SMOKING

Smoking was originally developed as a preserving method before the advent of refrigeration, but the wonderful effect that it has on flavour and texture means it's still a popular way of preparing food, including fish. The key to guaranteeing a good result is high-quality fish – the rest is down to the individual smoker's art.

Smoked fish comes in three forms: fully cured cold-smoked fish; partially cured cold-smoked fish; and partially cured hot-smoked fish.

The first variety includes halibut, sturgeon, tuna, swordfish and marlin, but the best-known fish prepared in this way is salmon. Before smoking, it's packed in a salt cure (to which some brown sugar is traditionally added); this will draw moisture from the flesh, giving it a firmer texture. Afterwards it's cold smoked, which means that the temperature is never high enough to cook the flesh. The duration of the smoking process is decided by the smoke master according to the flavour they want to create, as is the type of wood used. Oak, beech or alder

Smoking has a wonderful effect on the flavour and texture of fish

are the usual suspects, but oak whisky-cask shavings, juniper, peat, heather, hickory or cherry wood can also be added to enhance the taste. Once smoked, it's ready to eat.

The second type – partially cured cold-smoked fish – include kippers (gutted, split herring), bloaters (whole, ungutted herring), Finnan haddies and Glasgow pales (two Scottish varieties of haddock fillets), cold-smoked cod (fillets) and lightly smoked salmon portions. Prior to being smoked, the fish is either soaked in brine or given a light sprinkling of salt. After smoking, all of them must be cooked (whether by grilling, poaching, frying or adding to a pie).

Hot-smoked fish, the third variety, is first partially cured then smoked in a hot kiln, which simultaneously cooks it. Fish prepared in this way include mackerel (often available sprinkled with flavourings such as pepper); Arbroath smokies (gutted haddock – though, originally, whiting was also used); buckling (similar to a smokie, but made with herring); eel (either whole or in fillet form); trout (in fillets); and salmon (either in fillet, sliced, cubed or flaked form).

Whichever smoking method is used, the smoker's aim is always to enhance the fish's intrinsic character, never to overwhelm it.

UNSUNG HEROES

In an effort to eat more seafood, it's easy to keep returning to the familiarity of cod and other popular types of white fish. But to do so is to miss out on some of the many less high-profile species – the unsung heroes of the fish counter – that are readily available and that make for great eating.

Whiting is one of them. Poached and served with parsley sauce and a creamy mash, it's a traditional British dish that fell out of fashion a while ago, but that very much deserves to be revisited. The same is true of mackerel, which is great simply grilled and served with a red onion, parsley and caper salad, dressed with lime juice and seasoned with black pepper, or the humble sprat, floured (together with a touch of paprika and salt) then fried. Gurnard is no great looker, but its flesh is deliciously firm, and tastes wonderful with Moroccan spices. Make some slashes in the flesh, then mix together some ground cumin, ground coriander, chopped fresh coriander and mint, plus some crushed garlic, paprika, lemon juice, olive and salt. Rub it into the fish and allow to marinate for at least half an hour before grilling.

Herring, or 'silver darlings', as they're affectionately known, are also woefully overlooked in this country. Their oily flesh eats incredibly well with a punchy Scandinavian-style mustard and dill sauce, or split and smoked – kippered, in other words (for more details, see page 118) – they make for a fantastic breakfast.

Though delicious, coley is comparatively underused

Just grill them with a little butter and serve with a squeeze of lemon and some brown or wholemeal bread on the side.

Finding a good alternative to cod is an increasing preoccupation among many British fish lovers. Two very worthy candidates are Alaskan pollock and Atlantic pollack; both belong to the same family as cod, and have the same succulent, firm white flakes and a similar flavour. Either of them works well instead of cod or haddock in dishes such as fish pie, as does coley, with its firm but tender flesh.

Experimenting with different species is not just for the adventurous home cook; most fishmongers will be able to demystify unfamiliar or neglected varieties by advising on the best ways to prepare and serve them. Their knowledge is a greatly under-exploited high-street resource, and one they're only too happy to share – now's the time to make use of it.

Mitch Tonks
Fishmonger, chef and founder of the FishWorks restaurant group

SUSTAINABILITY

As a modern, forward-thinking company, Young's believes strongly in doing things right, and we are acutely aware of our many corporate responsibilities. Inevitably, as we're a seafood specialist, these include making sustainable fisheries our top environmental priority, because we believe this is the area in which we can make the biggest difference.

Working within the industry and through our global network of suppliers, Young's is not afraid to challenge inappropriate practices or to change our sourcing policies to exert a positive influence. We have been involved with the Marine Stewardship Council since 1997 and are active within many industry environmental organisations. We also work closely with scientists, as well as with non-governmental organisations such as Greenpeace, the World Wildlife Fund and the Marine Conservation Society. In addition, we have invested in our own

research and sustainability initiatives, such as our 'boat to plate' traceability technology.

Every Young's purchasing decision is made only with a clear understanding that the environment has the capacity to support the fishing or fish-farming effort involved. Our seafood sustainability policy (Fish for Life™) is supported by our Ten Principles for Responsible Fish Procurement commitment, which governs the way we buy all our fish, be it wild-caught or farmed.

Fish is one of the last major sources of wild-caught food on earth. Recognising this, we will ensure that responsible fisheries remain at the top of the Young's agenda, to help ensure the long-term sustainability of seafood for future generations.

This is a dynamic, fast-changing environment and we recommend that you regularly visit our website **www.youngsfish.co.uk** which is continually updated.

AVAILABILITY, SEASONALITY AND QUALITY

Just like most natural ingredients, fish is subject to seasonal variations in both availability and quality. One of the most common causes of these variations is their spawning cycles, when certain textural changes can occur in the fish's flesh that negatively affect its eating quality. Once the fish has moved out of the spawning stage and returned to normal feeding and growth, its flesh will return to peak condition. The changes that plaice goes through are a typical example of this; during its spawning season, which starts in the New Year, its eating quality is noticeably diminished, and doesn't return to optimum condition until around May.

However, while it's relatively easy to give buying guidance for plaice, for many other species it's much less simple, as spawning seasons are not often

uniform, and can also vary year on year, depending on various environmental and oceanographic factors. At Young's, we are in continuous communication with fishermen so that we can rapidly respond to changing seasonal phenomena, ensuring that we catch fish when they're at their best. When it comes to farmed fish, it's a little easier, as stock can be managed in a way that avoids harvesting spawning fish and that allows production cycles to be planned in accordance with anticipated market demands. As a consequence, farmed fish is generally available all year round without any perceptible seasonal variation in quality or supply.

In an age when consumer choice is broader than it has ever been before, it's sometimes easy to forget that the availability of fresh seafood is subject to factors as fundamental as the state of the weather. Storms at sea can adversely affect supply, both from fishing boats and sea cage fish farms. Working patterns in the fishing industry also have an influence. Here in Britain, and in certain other fishing grounds around the globe, many fishing boats tie up for the Christmas and New Year holiday – so don't expect to be able to buy top-quality fresh fish over that period. Religious holidays in other parts of the world can also affect fresh supplies of fish such as tuna, as can monsoon seasons in the tropics.

Despite many people's continuing image of frozen fish as second best in comparison to fresh, it can, in fact, deliver excellent eating quality, as the fish ➤

will have been caught and frozen at the stage at which it's at the peak of its condition. Boats working in distant water fisheries will freeze fish on board within hours of it being caught, so that it doesn't have a chance to spoil during the long journey back to port. Many of the world's most sustainable fish stocks, such as Alaskan pollock and Arctic populations of Atlantic cod, are caught and frozen at sea in this way, ensuring that their quality isn't compromised.

But whatever time of year you buy fish, and whichever type you buy, the advice of a knowledgeable and experienced fishmonger is invaluable, so if you have one in your area, use them – they'll be able to give you the best guidance on what's good that day. Failing that, here's a guide on what to look for when making your selection:

HOW TO BUY FISH – A CHECKLIST
Fresh whole fish
• The eyes should be clear and convex, not sunken.
• The flesh should be firm and resilient to finger pressure.
• The fish should smell freshly and lightly of the sea. Don't buy fish with a strong 'fishy' or sulphurous odour, or that smells of ammonia. Oily fish like herring, mackerel and salmon should have a light, fresh oil smell, like linseed oil. If they smell of rancid oil, don't buy.

Fresh fillets

• The surface of the fillet should be moist, with no signs of discolouration.

• The texture should be firm, with no mushiness. Some separation of the muscle flakes (caused by the filleting process) is completely normal, but it shouldn't be excessive.

• As with whole fish, the smell should be fresh and light, with no 'off' odours.

Live bi-valves (including mussels, clams and oysters)

• The general rule of not buying bi-valves during any month spelled without an 'r' (ie May to August) still holds true, as this is the spawning season and quality will be poorer. When raw, the shells should be closed tight. Any slightly open shells that don't close up in response to a few light taps should be discarded. When cooked, the shells should open — discard any that don't.

Frozen fish

• Avoid frozen fish with a 'cotton wool' appearance to its surface — it's the result of cold storage dehydration, or 'freezer burn', as it's otherwise known.

Creating the Young's Lexicon of Fish has been a rewarding experience. We are confident it will enrich your understanding and enjoyment of texture, taste and aroma of the many species available and, more importantly, serve as a catalyst to encourage you to try something different when choosing seafood.

Young's would like to thank all those who helped in bringing this project together, from the tenacious team at Young's who sourced the fish for tasting, to our very dedicated tasting panel and also to Jenny McIvor for help in bringing the panel's descriptions to life.

We would also like to thank Mitch Tonks and Wordbird for their additional contributions, Archant Dialogue for the creation, design and production and Sherbert Lemon and Wild Card for direction and co-ordination.

Photography used from Young's Seafood 2005, John Angerson; photograph of "Columbia", courtesy Trident Seafoods; photograph of Mitch Tonks, Peter Cassidy; Maldives photograph Nick Scott for Doner Cardwell Hawkins; Fishmongers, Nick Turner for Alamy; Lisa Romerein for Getty.

Taxonomy: Dr David Wilcockson, University of Wales, Bangor

IMPORTANT NOTE
This lexicon is intended as a guide to the sensory characteristics of a selected number of fish and seafood species. It is not intended as an indication of sustainability or as a recommendation to buy, and not all of those listed are sold by Young's. A few species that, owing to their stock status, should currently be regarded with particular caution are indicated in the text by this symbol: †.

For those who are concerned about the status of fish stocks and are wondering if the eating of fish is an ethical choice, the message is simple: buy fish with care, invest some time in examining the facts and select products bearing the Marine Stewardship Council certification logo wherever possible.

Choose a brand that you know you can trust. The Young's Fish for Life policy is an independently verified audit process that ensures we market only responsibly caught seafood. You can find more details at www.youngsfish.co.uk.

NOTES

NOTES